Reindeer

by Caroline Arnold

illustrated by Pamela Johnson

SCHOLASTIC INC.

New York Toronto London Auckland Sydney

Spring is coming to the far north. Short days are growing longer, and underneath the snow new grass is beginning to sprout.

The reindeer are restless. Clickety-clack, clickety-clack, they tap their hard hooves on the icy ground. They know that it is time to leave for their summer pastures.

The reindeer herders are packing food, tents, and clothing. They will lead the herds of reindeer on the long journey north. They will go to the vast, treeless plain of the Arctic tundra.

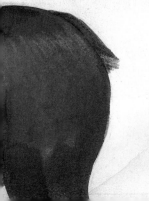

Reindeer are native to northern Europe and Asia. A few reindeer also live in Alaska and Canada. They were brought there from Europe about 100 years ago.

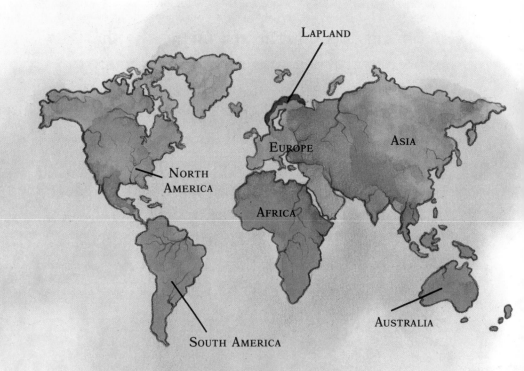

In ancient times reindeer were wild animals. People hunted them for their meat and hides. They ate the meat and used the hides to make clothes, blankets, and tents.

About 1500 years ago people began to catch wild reindeer and tame them. People taught their reindeer to carry things and to pull sleds. They used reindeer milk for drinking and for making cheese.

Over time wild reindeer became scarce. Now most reindeer are tame.

Reindeer are closely related to caribou (KAR-i-boo). Caribou live in North America and Siberia.

Caribou have longer faces than reindeer and they are bigger. Caribou stand 54 to 60 inches tall, and weigh up to 700 pounds. Reindeer stand about 43 inches high at the shoulder. Males may weigh 300 pounds or more. Females weigh slightly less.

The main difference between reindeer and caribou is that caribou are wild. Native people of North America hunt caribou, but they do not keep them as domestic, or tame, animals.

Caribou often form huge herds of thousands of animals. They migrate, or travel, long distances between their winter and summer homes.

Arctic winters are long and cold. Strong winds blow, deep snow covers the ground, and the temperature often falls below zero.

Reindeer and caribou are well suited to life in this harsh climate. Thick coats keep their bodies warm and dry. Even their noses are covered with hair!

Sturdy legs and broad feet help reindeer and caribou walk across the icy snow. Each foot has a wide hoof. It acts like a snowshoe to keep the foot from sinking into soft snow or mud. A large prong at the back of each foot is called the dewclaw. It digs into the snow and helps keep the foot in place.

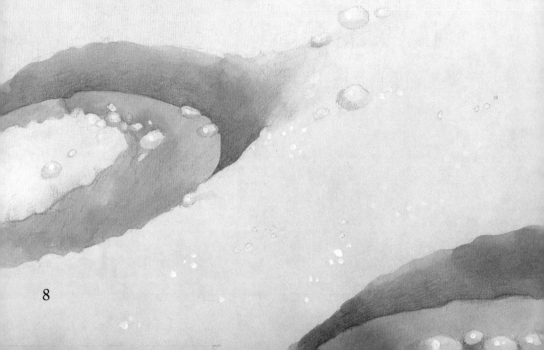

Today reindeer are found in the northern parts of Norway, Sweden, Finland, and Russia. This region is known as Lapland. The people who live there call themselves the Sami.

For hundreds of years the Sami people have herded reindeer. They invented skis so they could follow their reindeer across the snow.

In winter the Sami and the reindeer live in the forests. The reindeer eat a plant called reindeer moss. Reindeer moss helps keep the reindeer alive. But it does not have much protein. The reindeer need protein to grow and to make their muscles strong. The plants that grow on the tundra are rich with protein. So, as soon as the snow begins to melt in spring, the Sami and their reindeer leave for the tundra along the coast.

In Lapland today, several Sami families may combine their herds for the journey north in the spring. Some of the people and the pregnant female reindeer leave first. A week or two later, the rest follow them.

Some of the reindeer are harnessed to sleds that are loaded with supplies. The other reindeer follow each other in long lines across the snow. Dogs help the herders keep their reindeer on the right path.

The Sami and their reindeer may travel 200 miles or more from their winter home to their summer pastures. The trip takes many days. Their path goes through forests, into valleys, over mountains, and across icy cold rivers.

Soon after the female reindeer arrive at their summer pastures, they are ready to give birth.

A baby reindeer is called a calf. The mother reindeer usually has just one calf each year. (Twins are sometimes born.) A newborn calf weighs eight to ten pounds and is covered with a sleek, dark coat. Its mother leans over to lick it. Soon the calf is clean and dry.

Within an hour of its birth, the calf struggles to stand. Then it snuggles close to its mother. It drinks milk from her udder. The mother's large body keeps her calf warm, and her milk helps it to grow.

In two weeks the young calf doubles its weight. By the time it is three months old, it will stop nursing. Then the calf will eat plants like the older animals do.

Soon the rest of the reindeer join the females and their new calves. They are tired after their long journey. Their bodies are thin after a long winter without much food.

Summer days above the Arctic Circle are very long. In June and July the sun never sets. All the plants grow quickly. The reindeer eat and eat. Soon their bodies grow strong and firm again.

A reindeer has no upper teeth in the front of its mouth. It chews with its flat back teeth. After chewing its food, the reindeer swallows. Later, the reindeer coughs the food back up. When the reindeer chews the food again, we say it is chewing its cud. Then the cud is swallowed and digested.

A young reindeer's legs are wobbly at first, but they quickly grow strong. The calf must follow its mother as she moves about to feed.

If a calf lags behind, its mother turns and bobs her head. At the same time she grunts, as if to say, "Follow me."

"Maa, maa," bleats the calf and hurries to catch up.

As the reindeer calves get bigger, they start to explore. Sometimes they chase each other or butt heads. These exercises help their muscles grow strong.

Each Sami family knows its own reindeer by notches on the reindeer's ears. One job during the summer is to catch the calves and mark their ears.

By fall, a reindeer calf weighs 100 pounds or more. Much of what the reindeer eats in summer is stored in the body as a layer of fat. The fat keeps the reindeer warm and it provides energy during the long winter months.

A reindeer's coat also provides warmth. The fine hair next to the skin is short and curly. It forms a soft, inner lining. Over that lies a layer of long, coarse outer hairs.

These straight hairs are hollow, like tiny straws. The air trapped inside them keeps the reindeer warm. It also helps the reindeer to float when it swims across lakes and rivers.

Each spring the heavy outer hairs fall out in large clumps. The reindeer does not need them in summer. By fall, a new thick coat will grow in. Then the reindeer will be ready for cold weather.

When a reindeer calf is about three weeks old, two small bumps appear on the top of its head. These are the beginnings of antlers. By the end of the summer they will be spikes about 12 inches long.

Antlers are grown and shed every year. Each new pair is larger and heavier than the one before. The antlers of an older male reindeer may weigh 60 pounds! They may be as much as four feet wide and five feet high.

The new antlers are covered with a soft, tender skin called velvet. Blood in the velvet helps the antlers to grow. When they have finished growing, the velvet falls off. Then you can see the hard, bony antlers underneath.

Reindeer and caribou belong to the same family as deer, moose, and elk.

Antlers grow only on *male* deer, moose, and elk. But *both* male and female reindeer and caribou grow antlers. The antlers of males are larger than those of females. Male reindeer and caribou also have a large ruff, or mane, of long hair hanging around the neck.

In late summer and early fall, the crash of antlers can be heard across the tundra. It is mating time. This period is called the rut. The male reindeer butt heads as they fight for the right to mate with the females.

After mating, a female reindeer is pregnant for seven months and one week. She will give birth to her new calf in the following spring. By then her calf from the year before will be able to take care of itself.

When the rut is over, the male reindeer lose their antlers. Female reindeer keep their antlers through the winter. They shed them in the spring.

In the winter, reindeer dig holes in the snow to find food. A mother reindeer shares her hole with her calf. Scientists think that antlers may help the mother defend this spot from other hungry reindeer. Then she and her calf will get enough to eat.

eagle

arctic fox

By early fall, Arctic days are short.
The air grows cool, and frost covers the
ground. Soon winter blizzards will come.
The reindeer herders fold their tents and
pack their belongings. It is time to go to
their winter homes.

On the journey, the Sami must watch
out for predators. These are animals that
might attack the reindeer calves. Predators
of reindeer include foxes, wolverines,
eagles, and lynxes.

Reindeer herding is a business for the Sami. Twice a year they sell some of their reindeer to be used for meat. The money helps them buy things they need. The Sami may also kill a few of the animals for their own use.

For hundreds of years reindeer herding has been a way of life for the Sami. In the rest of Europe and in Asia, other groups of people herd reindeer, too. Each group has its own reindeer-herding traditions.

Today the lives of the reindeer herders are changing. For many herders, snowmobiles and airplanes have replaced skis. Some people prefer to keep their reindeer on farms all year long. Other people have moved away to towns and cities and no longer depend on reindeer for a living.

Only a few people still follow the traditional reindeer-herding life. Like their ancestors, they follow the rhythm of the seasons with the reindeer.

Index

About the Author

Photo by Richard Hewett

Caroline Arnold is the author of more than eighty books for children, including award-winning titles such as *Koala*, *Saving the Peregrine Falcon*, and *Dinosaur Mountain*. When she was growing up in Minneapolis, Minnesota, she spent her summers at a camp in northern Wisconsin. That is where she first developed her interest in animals and the out-of-doors.

Today she goes to zoos, museums, and wildlife parks as part of the research for her books. Ms. Arnold lives in Los Angeles, California, with her husband, who is a neuroscientist, and their two children. Ms. Arnold also teaches part-time in the Writers' Program at UCLA Extension.

If You Want to Read More About Reindeer:

Arctic Lands, by Henry Pluckrose (Gloucester Press, 1982).

Biography of an American Reindeer, by Alice Hopf (Putnam, 1976).

The Caribou, by Lorie K. Harris (Dillon, 1988).

Reindeer Trail, by Berta and Elmer Hader (Macmillan, 1959).

Library of Congress Cataloging-in-Publication Data

Arnold, Caroline.
Reindeer / by Caroline Arnold; illustrations by Pamela Johnson.
p.   cm.
Includes bibliographical references and index.
Summary: Follows a herd of reindeer from the forest where they
spend the winter to their summer grazing place on the tundra of
Lapland where their calves are born.
ISBN 0-590-46943-6
1. Reindeer — Juvenile literature.   [1. Reindeer.]
I. Johnson, Pamela, ill.   II. Title.
SF401.R4A76   1993
636.2'94 — dc20   93-12981
                                                      CIP
                                                      AC

12 11 10 9 8 7 6 5 4   4 5 6 7 8/9

Printed in the U.S.A.   23

First Scholastic printing, October 1993

Book design by Laurie McBarnette